A Playbook For a Successful Financial Planning Career

Getting the Job Done and Building Solid Client Relationships

Alan R. Leist, Jr., CFP®

Second Edition

ISBN: 978-1-7377020-3-0

Made in the United States of America

TABLE OF CONTENTS

Disclosure

The views outlined in this book are those of the author, and not of Strategic Financial Services, Inc., and should not be construed as individualized or personalized investment advice. Any economic and/or performance information cited is historical and not indicative of future results.

Different types of investments involve varying degrees of risk, and there can be no assurance that the future performance of any specific investment, investment strategy, or product made reference to directly or indirectly in this book, will be profitable, equal any corresponding indicated historical performance level(s), or be suitable for a given investor or portfolio.

Investing in stocks include numerous specific risks including: the fluctuation of dividend, loss of entire principal and potential illiquidity of the investment in a falling market. Bonds are subject to market and interest rate risk if sold prior to maturity. Bond and bond mutual fund values and yields will decline as interest rates rise and bonds are subject to availability and change in price.

Case studies presented are based on actual clients; however, some of the information may have been changed or altered. These studies are provided for educational purposes only. Similar, or even positive results, cannot be guaranteed. Each client has their own unique set of circumstances so products and strategies may not be suitable for all people. Please consult with a qualified professional before implementing any strategy discussed herein.

No portion of these case studies is to be interpreted as a testimonial or endorsement of the author's, or his firm's, investment advisory services.

All information and statistics, including that used to compile charts and/or tables, is obtained from sources believed to be reliable, but we did not audit the information so we cannot verify the accuracy and do not guarantee reliability.

The information contained in this book is general in nature and offered only for educational purposes. No investment decisions should be based solely upon this book's contents. Moreover, you should not assume that any discussion or information contained in this book serves as the receipt of, or as a substitute for, personalized investment advice. This book is not a substitute for engaging a professional advisor for a personal consultation whereby all of your financial circumstances, risk tolerance, and investment objectives can be considered. To the extent that you have any questions regarding the applicability of any specific issue discussed above to your individual situation, you are encouraged to consult with the professional advisor of your choosing.

No warranty is made with respect to the accuracy or completeness of the information contained herein, and both the authors and the publisher specifically disclaim any responsibility for any liability, loss, or risk, personal or otherwise, which is incurred as a consequence, directly or indirectly, of the use and application of the contents of this book.

Prologue

For many years, the world of individual finance was limited in scope to prosperous individuals working with stockbrokers to build their base of investment assets. Little attention, if any, was devoted to the development of a "plan of action" geared toward helping these people, or anybody else for that matter, construct a program aimed at identifying and working toward achieving a set of specific goals. This publication is devoted to the financial planning process from the point of view of the practitioner. The needed background qualifications, licenses, technical training, and sales development initiatives are all discussed. These factors are then melded together with the steps involved in developing a robust, "stick-to-the-ribs" client base. For a more detailed discussion, please refer to *So You Want to Be a Financial Planner: Your Guide to a New Career* by Nancy Langdon Jones, CFP®.

To be successful in the financial planning profession, a combination of sales skills and the ability to transmit semi-complex technical information in an understandable format are essential. It is the planner's job to motivate people to take action on their financial lives. To do that often requires a gentle nudge or push. Please know that every reference to closing in the chapters that follow refer to that push or nudge that the clients need to get them on track. We are not really selling but rather counseling. At times, clients need this (closing) push and will be forever grateful to you for your efforts.

This publication is in no way intended to be all-encompassing but rather to provide some basic guidance as you enter or contemplate entering the financial planning field.

Alan R. Leist Jr., CFP®

Introduction

The Roaring Twenties and the Great Depression

The stock brokerage companies were the backbone of the interaction that consumers and industry had with financial markets for many years. The pinnacle of this interaction came in the 1920s, known as the mad hatter days or the flapper era, which is also when things began to change. For background purposes, there was a sense of unbridled optimism in the 1920s as stock prices soared and the wealthy simply attained more wealth by investing in the markets. The following is an examination of the conditions that prevailed in the financial markets through the 1920s and into the 1930s.

During these years, individual investors and institutions had the ability to use margin loans to feather their nests, meaning that they could borrow against the stocks they owned and use those funds to purchase more stocks. The borrowing limit was 90% of the value of the stocks held (loan-to-value relationship). While this worked well when stock prices were rising, the events that ensued were disastrous for the markets and stockholders and were a precursor to the Great Depression of the 1930s and early 1940s.

Stock prices did not continue to rise, and the impact on the world was severe. As the prices fell, investors were forced to sell their positions to maintain the 90% loan-to-value relationship, and the more they sold to maintain that ratio, the more stock prices continued to fall and fall fast. The investors, including individuals, many businesses, and financial institutions, had been taken by the "easy" profits available up to the point when stock prices began to fall. All investors who had margin loans were forced to not only sell their stock holdings to meet their margin loan obligations (margin calls) but other assets as well, often at prices significantly below market value, causing mass individual bankruptcies and business failures. Following that epic period of selling commonly known as the crash of 1929, national unemployment levels became extremely high, with tent cities and bread lines popping up across the country. My own father was born in 1923 and as a 10-year-old scrounged for as many odd jobs as he could, earning meager wages, perhaps 50 cents per week, which had to be turned over to his father to put food on the table.

For perspective, the Dow Jones Industrial Average rose from 200 in 1928 to nearly 380 through 1929, dropping in value by more than 50% in 1930, with continuing drops thereafter. The attached chart (see appendix, part A) puts in perspective the incredible decline in value experienced by the Dow Average and the number of years it took for a recovery to begin. During this time, the investing public, businesses, and individuals simply did not have money to invest and were undoubtedly afraid of the stock market in any case. Even today, you run might across people or families shaped by the Depression era who are incredibly careful with their money, avoiding what they perceive as a risky strategy so as not to experience what they or their families did in the 1930s, and who can blame them?

Fortunately for all of us, regulation of the financial markets has increased significantly over time. For one thing, the use of margin loans has declined tremendously and are now limited to 40–50% of a portfolio's value. Even beyond these measures, there are trillions of dollars invested in retirement plan accounts that are not allowed to use margin loans for the purpose of purchasing more securities. In different terms, the equity in the financial markets today is a huge buffer against a collapse like the one that occurred in the 1920s. You can see from the list of securities laws provided here (see appendix, part B) that there were several bills and regulations put into effect from the 1930s onward to protect the investing public from rampant speculation and unregulated security offerings.

In particular, the Securities Act of 1933 was a watershed moment in the creation of investor protection regulations, requiring basic safeguards like the disclosure and registration of securities offerings with the federal government. These regulations were previously handled at the state level but, with the passage of the 1933 act, federal uniformity was instituted. Another extremely important piece of legislation was the Investment Company Act of 1940. This law was the catalyst allowing for the sale of mutual fund shares and shares of unit investment trusts to be regulated and sold to the public, opening opportunities for the general population to participate in financial markets. As a result of this, the doors to the investment world were opened again, and the stock market began to be looked upon favorably by many.

This shift was slow, taking three or four decades after 1940 until the post-Depression generation attained the confidence to really begin investing again. Today's economy is enormous compared to the late 1920s, as the amount of money invested in financial instruments now totals trillions of dollars. Investment assets are held by large segments of the population, through retirement plans and individual investments, and throughout other segments of the service industry, industrial complex, and not-for-profit organizations in operating and reserve funds.

We can look comfortably toward the future with the help of the previously mentioned regulations, an enormous diversity in the types of investment vehicles available, and the continued growth that seems promised by the application of innovation and technology in the finance industry. But let us not get ahead of ourselves. Before confidence could be fully restored in the financial markets, more trouble loomed ahead.

WWII: Another Shoe Drops

As if the Great Depression was not enough in its own right, at the end of the 1930s, Nazi Germany's leader, Adolf Hitler, developed and began to implement a plan to totally take over the continent of Europe, and perhaps a lot more, with the assistance of the Italian military. On September 1, 1939, the Nazis invaded Poland, first from the east and then from the west. This initiative marked the beginning of World War II, which lasted six years and one day, ending with the total surrender of Japanese forces on September 2, 1945. Prior to that date, the tide began to turn for the Allied Forces on June 6, 1944, with the successful D-Day landing in Normandy. There were a substantial number of lives sacrificed that day to thwart Nazi aggression, but this sacrifice saved the world from a tyrannical regime that would have created living conditions that are very different from what we have today. After the success at Normandy, the Allied forces, led by the United States, Great Britain, and France, made an unrelenting effort to turn back the Nazi takeover of much of the European continent. These forces had many successes in their united efforts, thus rendering the Nazis incapable of continuing their assault on humanity.

During this effort, the horror of the Nazi concentration camps came to the surface. The Nazis expressed their sick views on "ethnic cleansing" by rounding up millions of the Jewish population and shipping them to concentration camps where many lives were lost in unconscionable ways. The very welcome end of the war was preceded, in April of 1945, by Adolf Hitler and his wife taking their own lives by ingesting cyanide pills and finally with Hitler ending hisown life with a gunshot to the head. Undoubtedly, Hitler's demise demoralized the already weakened Nazi forces, bolstering the Allied effort to end the war. Leaders of the Allied Forces, Winston Churchill, Franklin D. Roosevelt, future president Dwight D. Eisenhower, and Charles de Gaulle, helped define the coming of a new world.

The feeling of joy around the globe following the Nazi defeat was palpable, and the soldiers who returned home to their families were greeted with overwhelming elation and gratitude. The photograph included here (see appendix, part C) of the Times Square celebration in New York City on the day that victory was declared over Japanese forces is one of the most famous in history and is so reflective of those feelings. [1] Many of the young people that went to war to defend our country had never been married or, at the very least, had not married until they were deployed in the service of our country. As a result, the end of the war brought forth a whole new generation of families and children in the immediately ensuing years. This generation of children came to be known as the baby boom generation. With the 1929 stock market crash, the Great Depression of the 1930s, World War II, and the horrific specter of concentration camps in the rearview mirror, the people who lived through these very disturbing periods were conservative in their approaches to life and financial affairs.

[1] Photo by Alfred Eisenstaedt, August 14, 1945

The New Era

Following the events detailed in the previous section, a growing sense of entrepreneurship began emerging in the United States, and as the baby boom generation grew, the number of innovative initiatives grew with them. Significant developments in the decade that followed WWII include the first computer, named ENIAC, in 1946; first commercial computer (UNIVAC I) in 1952; color televisions (invented in the late 1940s and introduced commercially in 1953); the jet engine for military use in 1948 and commercial transportation in 1952; along with nonstick pans; the hula hoop; Fortran—the first universal computer language—and Mr. Potato Head (under attack today in an effort to diversify). This decade, which was chock full of big-time advancements, was followed in the 1960s with the handheld calculator, touch-tone telephones, the first computer mouse, Valium, AstroTurf, ATMs, heart transplants, the first supersonic airplane, and the first lunar landing. This phenomenal period of invention continued into the 1970s, during which time many more developments were added—the Internet, email, VCRs, mobile phones, the Apple computer, the Rubik's cube, digital cameras, Sony Walkman, and genetic engineering, among others. There were many more developments not mentioned here from the mid-1940s through the end of the 1970s that had the effect of validating the prowess of the returning war heroes and the baby boom generation, which was coming to adulthood during this period.

As the baby boom generation maturation process continued, so did the pace of innovations, and as a result, the United States economy began to take significant steps toward growth and prosperity. While initial progress was slow, the economy did pick up steam as the 1940s drew to a close. Understandably, there was great reluctance on the part of a generation that suffered through war and economic depression to confidently save and invest, but the irrepressible American ingenuity that led to some of the incredibly significant inventions mentioned above also advanced the economic power of our great country.

From this very impressive list of innovations, three of the most notable are the jet engine, which made the entire world more accessible; computer technology, which advanced the efficiency of industry; and the television, which brought the population together with news, entertainment, and sporting events, now made accessible to the masses.

In the late 1970s, the baby boom generation started earning enough money to save and start planning for their futures. The parents of this generation, however, were looking to retire with a combination of Social Security, company- and government-sponsored pension plans, and any savings they could muster. Out of all this, a new industry was born called financial planning—an industry that is supported today by the College for Financial Planning, which had very rudimentary beginnings in 1972 but has matured significantly since then. The College for Financial Planning introduced the Certified Financial Planning curriculum in 1985, which is the gold standard today for a legion of planning professionals. In 2019, there were a total of 310,000 financial planners in the United States, of which around 80,000 carry the Certified Financial Planner (CFP®) designation, and that number is growing quickly.

Is a Financial Planning Career for You?

With 80,000 or more Certified Financial Planners (CFP®) and a legion of others who do not have this qualification working to provide service to the citizens of the United States, do you really want to become a financial planner? The most recent statistics say that, in addition to Certified Financial Planners (CFP®s), there are another 220,000 advisors [2] serving less than 25% of the adult (18+) population. Financial planning for the balance of the populace consists of do-it-yourselfers, people who are mostly or often living paycheck to paycheck, and those who simply cannot relate to what financial planning can mean to them and their future.

These numbers simply say that, while the financial planning industry has grown, there is still significant opportunity for future growth. If the US adult population numbers 250 million people, and there are 300,000 advisors [3], then there is a market for each advisor, including CFP®s and other practitioners, that totals more than 830 individuals. Breaking that down further, there is a market opportunity of more than 3,100 people for every Certified Financial Planner (CFP®). These statistics require some watering down, as not all the financial advising population is fully engaged in the planning process nor are all of these 250 million adults actual candidates for planning services. Suffice it to say that, even with watering down the numbers, there is a great market available for anyone who wants to do the work and take the risk. Looking a little deeper, the average financial planner earns about $125,000 per year [4], a tidy sum for a job seeker.

What characteristics should someone have who is interested in a financial planning career? First, a definition of financial planning might run something like this: "Fully aligning oneself with clients' interests by preparing, implementing, frequently reviewing, and adjusting plans aimed at helping the clients achieve their goals." That sounds straightforward and easy, but good financial planners must have a distinct set of skills to succeed:

1. They must have the ability to understand complex concepts, communicate them effectively to clients, and employ them as needed.
2. Effective planners must also be able to market their services so that there are clients to plan for.
3. Effective planners often must play the role of life counselor for their clients, helping them navigate through a myriad of life's issues.

Many people have one or two of these skills but not the other(s), which would make success exceedingly difficult to achieve. All the potential planners in the world who lack problem-solving capacities, identification skills, and technical knowledge are in for truly short careers. Additionally, there are a whole slew of people who have a product-knowledge-signaling alphabet soup after their names, like CFP®, CLU®, ChFC®, CFA®, CMT®, and on and on. These people have studied hard and know a lot about a lot, but without clients to serve, teaching might be their best choice. The third factor noted above is really dependent on the planner's DNA, so to speak—helping people is a key ingredient to long-term success, and if you do not have the desire to do that, potential clients can often see right through it.

---

[2] U.S. Bureau of Labor Statistics, [3] U.S. Bureau of Labor Statistics

[4] Forbes Magazine, research by Andrew DePietro, Feb. 2019

Another quality that is extremely helpful for launching a career in this field is a very thick skin. In searching for clients, particularly in the first five years or so, frequent rejection is an inevitability. Many people with planning stars in their eyes have succumbed to the humiliation of being rejected repeatedly.

One must be convinced not to take this personally and develop the conviction that, when clients sign on, they are not doing you a favor but have just done one for themselves that will truly transform their lives.

Even with consideration of these difficulties, a career in financial planning can be extremely rewarding. In most cases, the financial planning part comes in second to helping clients with many related concerns throughout their lives. Numerous people have thanked me profusely for helping them on so many issues. Those words of gratitude are often accompanied by a heartfelt handshake, hug, or tears.

Getting Started

If you have made the decision to venture into the field of financial planning, there are a few basic things you should do to begin launching your effort. First, there are two avenues that can be taken when you get started:

1. Operate as an individual practitioner - "hang out your own shield"
2. Work for a financial planning firm.

Both options should be explored completely.

"Hanging out your own shield" will require sufficient capital to launch your career, which includes feeding your family for an extended period, setting up an office, launching a sales and marketing campaign, paying for any other employees, managing payroll, providing employee benefits and a myriad of other expenses. The benefits of going in this direction are your complete independence, freedom of operation, being your own boss and, if successful, building a very salable business that has paid you handsomely along the way. Self-awareness and assessment are important here. Be honest with yourself. Seriously ask, "Do I have the ability to take this from ground zero to success?" Financial and emotional considerations must be considered in this questioning process. The independent financial planner must decide how to be compensated. The alternatives range from fee only, to fees plus commissions or commissions only. The fee-only model is prevalent today as it eliminates many built-in conflicts that couldarise or at least be perceived to do so with the addition of "selling "a product. The independent planner should research fees that are being charged in the marketplace and develop a comfortable model to work with.

Going to work for an established financial planning firm eliminates many of the above considerations. The firm, however, will require your commitment both from a financial point of view (compensation) and in having the firm own your clients. In the final analysis, it comes down to the planner's comfort level in taking the risk of "hanging out your own shield" versus working for a firm that provides you with the tools to succeed and in return exercises control over your future. In this instance, the firm a planner goes to work for will determine the compensation plan which often begins with a training salary for a specific period followed by a salary and perhaps a "bonus" based on production. There are numerous plans in effect, but know that, although the security involved for the planner is important, it does require sacrificing independence. The new planner will then use the established firm's compensation and investment platform.

One approach is not better than the other here, but your assessment requires honest introspection throughout the decision-making process.

In either case, the next step is to educate yourself about the fundamentals of the planning process. Perhaps the best way to do that is to join and enroll in the College for Financial Planning to begin studying for the Certified Financial Planner (CFP®) designation. This program is structured in modules and gives you exposure to all the necessary ingredients needed to plan for your clients. These modules include the following:

- Professional Conduct and Regulations
- General Principles of Financial Planning

- Education Planning
- Risk Management and Insurance Planning
- Investment Planning
- Tax Planning
- Retirement Savings and Income Planning
- Estate Planning
- Financial Plan Development

Before you begin the Certified Financial Planner (CFP®) application process, you must pass the CFP® board's candidate fitness standards and earn or plan to earn a bachelor's degree from an accredited college or university within five years of earning your certification.

You have the option of enrolling in an online course, of which there are several, with the possibility of completing the curriculum in as little as 9 months. Many people dive in and do it themselves in a much shorter period. Without question, there is nothing in this business that can top actual on the job training, but this nine-module session is a great introduction to the field. Most importantly, it arms the potential new planner with a list of things to look for in planning for their clients and some techniques that are tried and true.

There are numerous designations that a new or seasoned planner can seek, but the CFP® "degree" is the most useful. A recap of the available programs can be easily accessed online. *So, You Want to Be a Financial Planner* by Nancy Langdon Jones, CFP®, is also an excellent resource.

Regardless of the platform selected, the CFP® program provides a foundation for all planning initiatives. In addition to the CFP® training, it is advisable for new planners to acquire licenses in the securities field so that they can transact business on the New York and NASDAQ stock exchanges. It is generally recommended that the planner study for and obtain a Series 7 securities license, which provides the broadest access to the markets that planners might deal with. While the material learned in the Series 7 education process is not necessarily planning-oriented, like in the CFP® program, you do get some insight into the workings of the securities markets, which is extremely helpful. In addition to these licenses, it would be advisable to study and apply for licenses in the insurance field, including life, disability, accident, and health. There are many variations in the types of insurance coverages one can use for their clients' benefit, and the CFP® program gives you the basic information on them. Please note licensing requirements vary by state and the prospective planner should comply with his/her state's requirements. In addition, the business model selected will also dictate the necessary license requirements.

Effective planners must have in-depth technical knowledge to properly serve their clients and the Certified Financial Planner (CFP®) Program gives the planner an excellent foundation. In addition to the technical knowledge, planners must also be able to sell themselves and their planning process to attract clients and motivate them to act. The rest of this publication will be focused on building solid client relationships. A program called Professional Selling Skills™ is a wonderful place to start. This program overs many aspects of a successful sales process, including

- Owning the conversation
- Asking the right questions
- Resolving customer concerns
- Closing.

The most important skills planners can employ include knowing what questions to ask, LISTENING to the answers, and having such a thorough knowledge of the planning process that they can steer the conversation and ask pertinent follow-up questions. Listening is perhaps the biggest key, which helps immensely with identifying the issues that you can help clients work through.

In summary, studying for and earning the CFP® designation, coupled with an effective sales training program, equips you to succeed. But the hard part is yet to come—attracting clients to work with you and embracing the rejection you will undoubtedly experience as a part of the process.

As a point of emphasis, The College for Financial Planning Code of Ethics which lays out practice standards and procedures in a very effective way and should be assiduously adhered to by anyone practicing in the financial planning field.

Make Your Bed

In addition to the characteristics outlined in the previous section, retired US Navy Admiral William H. McRaven advises in his book [5] to start your day off by "making your bed."

This philosophy can be central to a planner's success. It revolves around organizing one's life by getting off to a solid start every day. McRaven's example of "making your bed" and carrying that through your daily activities should serve you very well and will be noticed by your clients and peers. "Making your bed" also entails keeping the room around you organized to support your activities, for example. The following are some essential "making your bed" suggestions.

Embedded in the "make your bed" analogy is the importance of organizing your work environment to ALLOW you to plan effectively. When you can control it, set up an office that is completely outfitted with all the tools you need to be successful. Make sure you have a solid and secure computer system. As an aside, outside consultants abound in the cybersecurity field and are well worth employing to protect your clients' data. Also, the programs used to run various forecasts for your clients, such as those centering on education or retirement planning, are extremely helpful. Our firm has found MoneyGuidePro™ to be an effective software package, allowing for the automation of the asset-tracking and forecasting processes. If you go to work for an established planning firm, take the time to find out what resources are available and learn how to use them.

Another essential part of "making your bed" is seeking out and employing a top-notch administrative assistant. A solid assistant is worth his or her weight in gold and will be a huge help in getting the basics done every day. When you make this hire, write up a job description that includes a range of tasks like setting up meetings, coordinating travel, making reservations, typing, and sending out letters, preparing meeting files, printing reports, sorting mail, and whatever other relevant activities you can think of. An important question to ask whenever a task surfaces, is "who else can do this for me?" Delegation allows the planner to be more productive and helps others learn through on-the-job training. A collateral benefit is the trust it builds with clients who know someone else is in the wings that can help them, if needed.

On another note, people will often come to you with a task they are supposed to do, a task I like to call "a monkey on their back," and these people will often try to pass the monkey off to you. But do not accept it; deflect it back to the perpetrator or someone else, if appropriate. **Always focus on the parts of the planning process that further client development** and develop those around you to aid with that central task.

Another piece of advice in the "make your bed" vein is that, when you are successful, you will be approached by many people who want to share your success by engaging you in any number of collateral projects or endeavors. Stick to your knitting and what is proven to work—it will pay off. The bottom line is: set everything up to maximize your productivity, as that will create more satisfied clients, and your financial rewards will reflect that.

---

[5] Make Your Bed: Little Things That Can Change Your Life...And Maybe the World, 2017.

The last concept to report on relative to "making your bed" is employing a consistent structure for meetings with clients, whether they be the initial get-together, follow-up meetings, or reviews. A predictable, repeatable meeting structure makes the whole process much easier on you and all your support people. Be consistent.

Successfully following the basic tenets of "make your bed" translates to "do the basics well every day," and this will result in a rewarding life for the planner.

Parts of this rewarding life will be filled with constant interaction with clients, employees, and other outside advisors. Client interaction requires an intense level of focus in that the planner's radar must be constantly on. Thorough premeeting preparation, asking the right questions, listening to the answers, and continual fact-finding, all coupled with keen sensitivity to the client's frame of mind and thorough follow up, keep a planner totally engaged. If your practice has the good fortune, due to your hard work, to hold 5–6 meetings per day, your "schmooze meter" may be off the scale when the day is done. I remember arriving home to hear, "don't you want to talk?" or "why are you being so quiet?" The answer is simple: I was on information and conversation overload. There were many nights when I simply declared that I needed an hour to decompress. This is all a part of building a successful and rewarding practice.

Thank you, Admiral McRaven.

RIPS

The personal and business tips outlined in the previous section are the bedrock elements of things to do to get a practice started. Once those characteristics and basic business formation practices are in place, the following, presented in a summary format, are suggestions to take those personal and business basics to the place where the rubber meets the road. While planners cannot control the financial markets, things that can be controlled are neatly encompassed by the following words: reputation, image, preparation and service (RIPS). While each of these is covered in the section that follows, the elements of RIPS are not necessarily presented in that order.

1. It is particularly important that planners do everything to promote and maintain a solid REPUTATION in the local community and the larger industry. Planners should consider volunteering for community activities that are of interest and conduct themselves in a manner that is perceived as positive by members of the community, clients, peers, outside advisors, and suppliers. Planners should also be fastidious in maintaining their own personal finances. A solid REPUTATION builds customer loyalty, generates referrals, and opens doors on so many fronts.

2. To help maintain one's REPUTATION, planners need not accept everyone who walks in the door just because it seems like the good thing to do from a reputation point of view. It is true that a bad apple can spoil the whole bunch. If a client has frequently changed planning firms, appears argumentative, cannot be managed regarding the acceptance of risks (e.g., "It is unacceptable for me to ever lose money"), resists the proposed fees vigorously, or voices any other contentious things, you are better off working with someone who appreciates you and the service. Don't try to push a wet rope up a hill. Likewise, if these things do develop in the course of any client relationships, suggest a divorce to these clients so they can find someone more aligned with their way of thinking. You will sleep better at night and your REPUTATION will remain intact, as you are maintaining a standard of excellence for the entire practice.

3. A positive IMAGE is essential. Planners should work to create a warm and welcoming environment to use in meetings with clients. The first person your client sees will be your office receptionist. This person creates the very first in-person impression of the business, setting the tone for the initial meeting and for every meeting thereafter. An accommodating personality is essential. The decor in your meeting area should be inviting and conducive to doing business. As an aside, you should consider avoiding business lunches, as it is difficult to close a case with lettuce in the way. A social lunch with a client is always acceptable, but do the business piece before or after lunch.

4. Further on the IMAGE front, the person who answers your telephone should be very accommodating. A rule of thumb is for the person answering to act as if he or she was expecting the client's call and is welcoming of it. The person who answers the telephone should also avoid bouncing the client hither and yon when trying to connect to an advisor or support person. The answerer should stay with the call all the way, never leaving the client hanging but offering a call back after giving the intended recipient two or three rings to answer.

5. Planners should also take care to maintain their personal IMAGE with exercise, a solid night's sleep, and a manner of dress that projects a business IMAGE. You never ever know who you are going to run into—getting on an airplane wearing a sweat suit and flip flops and expecting to engage in a conversation with a multimillion-dollar prospect who happens to be seated next to

you may not work well. Some of those people may not care, but why not err on the side of safety? As a side note, offering a beverage when the client enters is a wonderful way to make them feel welcome and certainly helps foster a positive IMAGE. In addition, posing the question, "do you need to use the rest room?" can go a long way, if appropriate.

6. Surround yourself with people who genuinely enjoy helping others, training them from scratch if necessary. The clients will deeply appreciate this trait and can sense quickly when someone does not have it. Keep the standard of helping others at an elevated level since it helps with IMAGE development and preservation.

7. Before you start your financial planning career, being well PREPARED is essential. Would-be planners should obtain as many of the prerequisite designations and licenses as they can, including Certified Financial Planner (CFP®), General Securities License Series 7, and life/health/disability insurance licenses. There are several more versions of the available security licenses, which can be found on the Financial Industry Regulatory Authority (FINRA) website (www.finra.org), but Series 7 is the most important. In addition, planners should make sure that licenses required by their state are obtained.

8. By way of PREPARATION, and if afforded the opportunity, every planner, both new and experienced, should spend some time in the operations area of the firm to fully understand the complexities and nuances of the client service activities. This helps tremendously in guiding clients through what kind of service they should expect.

9. Prior to every meeting, planners should take extra care to PREPARE for the client. This includes reviewing the client's personal data, preparing to ask questions about the client's life or family (this helps the meeting flow), and looking at previous follow-up letters, the current plan, the investment portfolio allocation and performance, open items you are working on, and anything else specific to that client. All of this helps to build ongoing client confidence.

10. One of the backbone principles of good SERVICE is the creation of FOLLOW-UP LETTERS. Every client meeting should be documented, with correspondence sent to the client and stored in the client's file. The words "past performance is not a guarantee of future results," "if we have missed anything, please let us know," and "if any of this is not correct, please let us know" are valuable tools. They serve as an excellent reminder for the topics covered and what needs to be addressed in the future. In addition, in a very litigious society, these letters offer an extra layer of protection to planners. A system should be in place that triggers a follow up from the appropriate person in the planner's firm so that things do not fall through the cracks. The importance of follow up, follow up, follow up cannot be overemphasized.

11. An important aspect of SERVICE can be referred to as THE SUNSET RULE—every employee, from the advisor to the operations people, should embrace and follow the sunset rule. If a client calls with a request for anything that cannot be addressed on the spot, and the person cannot get an answer before leaving for the day, call the client back before the end of the day and say you are working on the situation and will report back tomorrow. If the client calls within an hour or two before the end of the day, an "I will have the answer tomorrow" will suffice. Clients love this kind of service. Communicating in this manner from the outset of a relationship is also often a powerful closing tool, as people today are often shortchanged when it comes to service. Also, pay close attention to the menu of options presented when calling for service—hearing "dial 1 for service" and then "all of our representatives are busy now; your call is important to us, so stay on the line" is not the best for client relationships. A solid piece of advice is to always have a

real person answer the telephone and keep voicemail usage to a minimum, preferably for internal use only.

12. Further on SERVICE, planners should be unrelenting in following up on open items and attending to the myriad of details that inevitably present themselves. Planners should always confirm to the client when a problem is resolved, or a detail is taken care of; clients love this level of follow up.

13. Last and not the most or least important, but important nonetheless, is to thank the client for their business after every review meeting. In addition, if a client sends in a deposit for investment, a brief thank you note speaks volumes. If a client refers someone to you or the firm, always send them a handwritten thank you note. Clients appreciate all these little but meaningful gestures.

Reputation, image, preparation, and service working in concert have the impact of building client and employee confidence, and this will have an especially positive impact on business development.

Marketing and Sales

In addition to having a briefcase full of financial planning knowledge, successful financial planners must be able to attract clients to use this knowledge. Marketing and sales methods to follow are numerous, and financial planners must find and use those that fit them the best. Successful planners will construct a marketing plan and adhere to it religiously. An organized, consistent, regular approach to the process of getting clients is essential to success. After several months of trying a particular approach with only limited or qualified success, adjusting and fine tuning are certainly appropriate, but remember to give it time at the outset.

Before we enter the arena of sales and marketing techniques, one of the most important qualities that financial planners can have is the ability to face repeated rejection. This has been said before, but it cannot be overemphasized since it marks a serious obstacle to a successful planning career. Many potential clients who are approached for financial planning services generally do not have any idea what they are being presented with, and the knee-jerk reaction is often "not interested" or "I already have that." If the people approached do have knowledge of the financial planning process, they do not have any idea what you might bring to the table and therefore might say, "I am all set."

As a response, planners could say, "The financial field undergoes changes every day, and I would appreciate the opportunity to tell you how our firm handles those changes and adapts to the current environment. May I call you at some point to set up a mutually convenient time?" Financial planners must develop the mindset that getting an individual to agree to meet is a real opportunity to help the person, not the planner. The best decision a person can make is to get on a solid financial path for the future. Rejection will happen a lot more often than acceptance, and planners must not take it personally. The Professional Selling Skills training program will help equip planners to handle these issues. There are other programs, so get help in presenting and answering objections—the help will be worth its weight in gold. No matter the approach used, planners MUST become comfortable with and adept at handling negative reactions and rejections.

To focus more on the positive aspects of marketing and sales here, it is especially important to create opportunities to meet face-to-face with a prospective client. Meeting face-to-face allows planners to sell themselves and the process and directly ask for the client's business. Once successful in securing a face-to-face meeting, planners should have effective presentation materials and as stated before, ask for the business. Let us focus on inviting and securing that all-important face-to-face meeting. Here are a few strategies to consider:

1. Develop a website that presents a complete profile of the planner, the planner's firm, and the financial planning process in addition to a frequently asked questions section. The website should afford the opportunity to request information and an appointment.
2. Develop a social media profile that invites contact from people who might be interested in having a financial planning relationship. The goal of this may be as simple as steering people to your website.
3. Join one or several social or business organizations that provide an opportunity to network with a range of people, including peers who might be prospects for the planner's services.
4. Develop mailing lists and systematically send out around 25 introductory letters per week with a request for a meeting, following that up with a telephone call. Be prepared for rejection.

5. Run advertisements in newspapers, perhaps offering current perspectives on financial matters and directing readers to your website.
6. Ask current clients for referrals. As an example, consider the following: "Our firm has continually grown in an effort to meet your financial needs. Our ability to do that rests in developing new client relationships, so if you know anyone who might benefit from our services, we would appreciate the referral."
7. Develop a one-line response, an "elevator pitch," to use when someone asks, "What do you do"?
8. Consider running seminars on specific financial topics. Some planners even include lunch or dinner as encouragement for potential clients to attend.

There may be many other avenues to follow, and this list is not intended to be all-inclusive but can used for jump-starting your thinking. In every instance, planners must be readily prepared to explain what they do in a simple and straightforward manner—one or two sentences are all that's needed.

Whatever methods you choose to pursue clients, you must absolutely make it a consistent effort if you want to succeed. Be prepared to stick with your program and regularly execute your plan. If you intend to do something such as send introductory letters every two weeks, do it every two weeks without fail. As cold-hearted and unexciting as it might sound, the acquisition of clients is a numbers game, and a regular, consistent effort is required to be successful. This effort must include asking a prospective client for an appointment so that you can see if there is common ground for you to work together. In order to progress, you must become comfortable in asking for this appointment or meeting in a manner that suits your style. Always be prepared to answer questions and respond to objections. But ask, ask, and ask—and do not take rejection personally. As Wayne Gretzky reportedly said, "You miss 100% of the shots you don't take." [6]

It is important to see prospective clients face to face and marry that meeting together with effective presentation materials. If you are successful in setting up a meeting, a consistent structure to follow is extremely helpful in sharpening your presentation and closing skills. The following provides some suggestions for success:

1. Open with a strong statement like this: "My intention today is to give you enough information to see if we might be of assistance to you in working toward achieving your financial goals." Ask the prospective client if this makes sense and be prepared to respond.
2. If the prospective client agrees to that premise, then say, "If it makes sense to you, we would also like to gain some information from you to help us understand what directions we should go in. Does that make sense?"
3. To get started, begin within a brief history of the firm, an overview of its structure, and a summary of key personnel and responsibilities. Hit the service notion hard, saying something like, "We have no voicemail, we have a sunset rule, we send follow-up letters, we review meeting frequency, and we profile the team members who will provide service. Do you have any questions on that?"
4. An outline of the process should be provided so the prospective client knows what to expect. Please see the next chapter for more information.
5. It then makes sense to state, "For us to get started, we need to gather personal and financial information from you. We can start that today if you are comfortable," or, "If you would like to

[6] The [Yale] Dictionary of Modern Proverbs (2012), Charles Doyle, Wolfgang Mieder & Fred Shapiro

set up another meeting on a different day, we will send you a list of things needed to get started. What would you prefer?" Another effective way to close is by saying, "We are ready to proceed if you are. Just say the word."

6. Continually ask prospective clients if they have any questions at each stage of this meeting. This could be considered a series of soft closes.
7. It is then important to close for the next step in the process. The client may agree to the next step, which would be information gathering, goal setting, or plan presentation, if the necessary data is in hand.

The fact that the prospective client agreed to the first or second meeting signifies that a crucial step has been taken. Following the introductory session, the prospect might ask a simple question about, say, what do you charge for services? This can be viewed as a buying signal. Questions simply need to be answered, followed by "does that answer your question?" The client might also raise an objection such as "we are not ready to proceed at this time." The planner should then restate the objection and ask what the client's hesitation is. The handling of objections, along with many other effective sales techniques, are covered in the Professional Selling Skills training recommended earlier in this presentation. You are urged to avail yourself of this program. Not every introductory meeting will result in a client relationship, but this step is a major key in working toward building your base and, for that matter, your confidence.

An effective technique for the planner to employ, as said above, is to continually ask "closing" questions along the way. If done properly, closing on the plan implementation will follow logically and smoothly.

Good luck, but be ready to be rejected, be practiced in addressing questions and objections, take a moment to enjoy your successes, stick with your program every day, and your career will be on the go.

The Backbone of a Financial Plan

Before the topic of developing a financial plan is addressed, the information presented in this section is of great importance to the process. Many clients in their formative years are primarily interested in building their wealth through capital accumulation. This is to prepare for things like educating children and retiring comfortably. An overview of retirement plans, and a brief review of education funding as presented below could be considered the backbone of the capital accumulation process. As a result, this overview is put here in the manuscript preceding financial plan preparation.

To the great credit of American industry, company leaders recognized that economic development did not move forward without a well-trained and compensated work force. Part of that compensation came in the form of retirement plans. [7] The first such retirement vehicle, the defined benefit plan, was designed to provide the workforce with a predictable or even guaranteed lifetime retirement income. The defined benefit plan was introduced in the late 1800s, first by the American Express Company, and its popularity languished for over 50 years but really began to take root in the late 1940s and early 1950s. In 1970, 45% of the eligible workforce, which numbered some 26.3 million people (about the population of Texas today), was covered by defined benefit plans. That number held steady through 1990, when 43% of workers were still covered. At that point, companies began to reduce the use of these plans, such that today only 7% of the work force has this benefit. [8] The reasons why follow, but essentially reduced the level of responsibility employers had to provide retirement benefits.

The financial strength and security of defined benefit plans took a leap forward in 1974 with the passage of the Employment Retirement Income Security Act (ERISA), which put forth extremely strict regulations on these plans and forced their sponsors to adhere to stringent guidelines regarding solvency, enforced rigorous benefit protection for employees, and made the plans difficult to terminate in order protect employees. This piece of legislation was one catalyst in pushing many companies to change their retirement benefits strategies, moving from the companies themselves carrying the entire burden to a shared responsibility with employees.

Another key moment came with the passage of the 1978 Revenue Act, which established what today are called defined contribution plans. These plans, as adopted by businesses, were another central component in shifting the burden from the employer providing all of retirement benefits directly to the employee, either in part or totally. There are numerous defined contribution plan iterations, some involving a combination of direct contributions from the business, institution, or enterprise, some including money added by the employees and others that only involve employee contributions. Some of these plan types are profit sharing, 401(k), 401(k) with a match, 401(k) with a Roth option, simplified employee pension, Keough, SARSEP, SIMPLE IRA, 403(b), 457, and cash balance plans, among others. It does not make sense to go into all the nuances of each of these offerings, but planners should take time to become familiar with them and see where they might fit into a client's needs and goals. In the September 2020 primer, "Qualified Retirement Plans," Julia Kagan provides a helpful general overview on this topic.

[7] U.S. Pension Benefit Guaranty Corporation

[8] Russell Investments

As to the use of retirement plans, probably the most important skill that a planner can develop is the ability to recognize what type of plan would be best suited to assist business owners in achieving their financial goals. Once the plan type has been identified, presented, and agreed upon by the business or client, then the planner should consult with the experts in those plans to get it set up. The benefit of making tax-deferred contributions is that no income tax needs to be paid on the contribution at first but is instead levied when funds are withdrawn for retirement income. These popular and powerful retirement savings plans have roughly $37.2 trillion [9] in them today.

One very important addition to this array of planning alternatives took place in 1974 when legislation launching individual retirement accounts (IRAs) passed. Originally, deposits to these accounts were not tax deductible, but that all changed in 1981 with the Economic Recovery Tax Act, signed into law by Ronald Reagan. This opened up the IRA possibility for all workers (subject to income limitations) and allowed taxpayers to secure a deduction against their income for annual deposits up to the contribution limitations established and often modified by the Internal Revenue Service (IRS). In addition to the ordinary income tax savings associated with the deposit in an IRA, growth in IRA accounts accumulates on a tax-deferred basis. In other words, there will not be any income tax due until withdrawals begin and only on the amount of each withdrawal. There have always been limits placed on the amount that can be deposited, but contribution limits later went into effect for employees who were covered by retirement plans and hit certain income thresholds. IRAs hold assets totaling $3.2 trillion today.

A further, important addition to the IRA scene was the advent of Roth IRAs in 1997 through legislation introduced by Senators Bob Packwood of Oregon and William Roth of Delaware. Roth IRA contributions, as with contributions to traditional IRAs, are subject to certain limitations. Unlike traditional IRAs, however, the contributions to Roth IRAs are not tax deductible, but the earnings grow tax-free, and withdrawals are not subject to income taxation. Roth IRA accounts also pass to the beneficiary free of income and estate taxation and are not subject to required mandatory distributions at age 70 ½ (increasing to age 75 in 2024).

Suffice it to say, our United States government has been instrumental in enacting legislation to help workers accumulate money for retirement and putting regulations in place to keep businesses and professionals from abusing the plans. The retirement planning industry has burgeoned in the last 30 years, with providers making it easy for planners to implement plans for their clients. Still, however, all applicable rules must be followed carefully.

It is also very important to note that, beyond retirement plans, there are a host of options that can be used to accumulate money for future security. As a planner, it is important to find out how much people are going to need in retirement based on their projected living expenses. When this target, or series of targets, is established, the planner can then determine, assuming certain rates of return, how much needs to be saved to augment Social Security and retirement plan benefits. Often, a monthly target is set, and appropriate investment vehicles are recommended. These added investments do not allow for tax-deductible contributions but may offer some tax sheltering for the income generated. The range of options is enormous, comprising a laundry list that includes mutual funds, exchange traded funds, individually managed accounts, individual stocks, corporate bonds, municipal bonds, United States Treasury instruments, fixed annuities, savings accounts, certificates of deposit, variable annuities, and

[9] Merrill Lynch Wealth Management

guaranteed income annuities, to name a few. Beyond these, there are limited partnerships that invest in real estate, debt instruments, startup companies, distressed companies, and a variety of other areas or entities that Wall Street has conjured up. The planner should take the necessary steps to be educated about these options, be conversant in them, and be able to recommend suitable possibilities for clients.

The accumulation of funds to provide for the education of children generally involves a tailored savings plan which incorporates IRS Section 529 as an essential component. The planner should develop an understanding of 529 plans and incorporate them into an education funding strategy. The planner should work to develop a range of assumptions regarding a client's expectations as to the type of school, public or private, that a child might attend, the number of years of education to plan on and an agreed-upon annual cost using readily available date. Inflation rates and rates of return on the education funds need to be incorporated in the analysis. Suffice it to say, 529 plan accumulations may not cover the entire cost and may need to be supplemented with additional personal savings.

There are other less popular accumulation vehicles that can be explored as explained by Kathryn Flynn in an article written in 2018 titled "Ways You Can Save For College".

In summary and in regard to capital accumulation, the planner has a lot of options to choose from and needs to become fully versed in all of them to serve an increasingly sophisticated clientele. Beyond this, the competition is intense, and the effective planner will need a range of skills to develop a successful practice. I will address these issues in the next chapter.

The Planning Process

There are several stages in a client-planner relationship. They can be broken down as follows, each to be addressed in turn:

- Introductory Meeting
- Fact-finding
- Goal Setting
- Plan Preparation and Presentation
- Implementation
- Reviews and Follow Up

The Introductory Meeting

The introductory meeting is covered in depth in the previous chapter, but a bit more advice can be offered here. The skilled planner will develop the ability to handle this meeting in a natural and conversational way. Many firms will provide you with a "track to run on," but being comfortable with the process so it can be done in a relaxed manner is essential.

The skills involved in conducting the introductory meeting also include having enough familiarity with the process so that questions the prospective clients raise can be heard loud and clear and the planner can move with alacrity in answering them. The fundamental secret is for the planner to conduct numerous introductory meetings and, through those meetings, become skilled in the process. If necessary, have a solid set of presentation materials to work with. After the presentation is complete, you might ask simple questions about whether the client has been involved with the planning process before or has ever done any investing. These prompts are intended to get the client further engaged in the meeting.

To amplify on some of the suggestions made in the previous chapter, become conversationally adept at moving the process forward. For example, consider the following: "Our next step is to have an interview where we can set some goals and I can find out as much about your financial affairs as possible and get a sense as to things like your risk/reward tolerance and how assets should be left to your heirs. We can start that process today if you are comfortable. Or, if you would like to think about it and you agree we can help, set up another meeting. In either case, we will follow up with a list of documents we will need to begin our work." While this was covered in the previous chapter, practice saying it since it is a vital key to the engagement process.

Addendum to the Introductory Meeting

In many cases, when a couple is involved, one of the two has handled investments for both of them. The planner, however, needs to ask directly if both have been involved. If one answers, "No, I haven't," I always offer to make the short presentation outlined in the section that follows, Investing 101. In so many cases, even the "experienced" partner asks if they can take the presentation with them when they leave. To prepare for this, the presentation is provided on a plain sheet of paper for the meeting.

Fact-finding

If the client wants to start the process at the end of the introductory meeting, or if we have set a follow-up meeting for a later date so that the appropriate documents will then be in hand, the interview commences with a series of requests for information:

- Full names
- Dates of birth
- Social Security numbers
- Email addresses
- Residence addresses
- Business addresses
- Telephone numbers
- Preferred mailing address
- Current health picture
- A listing of assets and liabilities, including mortgage balances and interest rates
- Statements reflecting retirement plan balances—401(k), profit sharing plans, pension plans
- Determinations of how each asset is owned (for estate planning purposes)
- Children's names and ages, marital status, residence addresses and if needed, Social Security numbers and employment, names of grandchildren
- A sense of the financial acumen of each child—are they good with money?
- If a child is married, whether the marriage is in good shape
- Names and ages of siblings, nieces and nephews
- The client's investment experience and previous financial statements
- A sense of risk/reward tolerance—that is, how do you feel when the stock market declines in value?
- Are any parents still alive? If so, what is their marital and employment status? Do you expect any significant inheritances?
- Life insurance coverage (obtaining the actual policies or annual statements is important)
- Disability insurance coverage (again, obtaining documentation is critical)
- Current estate documents such as wills, trusts, health care proxies, living wills, and business agreements. This is absolutely essential!
- If the client is a business owner or partner in a professional practice, what is the exit strategy in the event of retirement or death? Is there a shareholder's agreement in place? If so, a copy is needed.
- What is the client's estimated value for his or her share of the practice? What provisions are in place for the client to realize that value upon leaving the business, becoming disabled, or passing away prematurely?

While I may have missed a few questions, all of this is aimed at getting a full picture of the client's situation and outlook. In addition, several business opportunities can develop from these questions, like those related to their children or business involvement. The planner must be attentive and fluid enough to look beyond the answer and find the meaning or opportunity that it presents.

If the firm the planner is working for has a template or form detailing which questions to ask in the introductory meeting, that is very helpful. If such a template doesn't exist, then planners should develop their own, making it increasingly simple as more and more new clients are met.

Goal Setting

Probably the single most important thing a financial planner can do is help the client set goals that reflect the client's values and establish the roadmap for the process to begin. Many times, the client will have to be guided through this process and will need some suggestions along the way. For example, the client may need to

- accumulate sufficient capital to be financially independent or retire at some point in the future (common ages are 55, 60, or 65)
- accumulate sufficient capital to educate children
- make sure that the survivors in a family are adequately protected in the event of a death or disability
- allow for the orderly and tax-effective transfer of assets to the next generation
- purchase a second home, support a relative, or afford any number of other projects or directives.

It is VITALLY important to repeat these goals back to the client after they are established and say, "Are those correct? Do any changes need to be made? Are you comfortable with them?" This sets the stage for the planning to commence, leading ultimately to the closing process. It is always good to review these goals with the client when you are presenting the plan and periodically thereafter. If you specifically address the client's goals when you present the plan, each one of these goals will then make sense and ease the process of implementation. Often, and particularly with younger clients, the capital to fully implement the recommendations set forth in the plan may not be available, and priorities must be set for the allocation of available cash.

One important point to remember is that the full implementation of a plan will be in the client's best interest, but the planner should approach the presentation with the thought that it may not be implemented in exactly the manner visualized. However, the plan is nevertheless an important start for the client and your relationship. Modifications and revisions may be done many times throughout the client-planner relationship.

Investing 101

At any point during a meeting with a potential client or when presenting the plan, particularly to those people who have not done any planning previously, the subject of investing will come up. I always ask if the people have had any experience with investments. In most cases, one or both partners will look quizzically at the presenter, at which point you might say, "I have a short and simple presentation that I like to call Investing 101. Would you like to see it?" Ninety-nine times out of one hundred, the answer will be yes, and that often comes from the (at least theoretically) experienced prospect.

At this point, I take a pad of paper and draw a line down the middle of it and say, in simple terms, when you invest money, you can either lend it to someone or buy ownership. The diagram included below illustrates this idea.

When you lend money to some entity, it promises to pay you interest and give you your money back at some point in the future. I then ask if they have heard the term "bonds" before (clients always nod), which means you are lending money to a corporation or a government agency. Depending on who you lend money to, the interest can be taxable or tax free. Other forms of lending might include bond exchange traded funds, bank savings deposits, certificates of deposit, fixed return annuities, or government securities, to name a few. When you lend money, the credit rating of the borrower is important, as you want to be paid your interest in a timely manner and get your money back when the instrument comes due, which is called maturity. Additionally, when you lend money, your return is not guaranteed and your capital is not protected if the issuer is unable to meet their obligations. It may be obvious, but money should not be lent based to low-rated credits.

When you buy ownership in something through a security, your fortunes rise and fall with the entity that you own. The most generic form of ownership is common stock, and in this case, your return comes through a rise in the price of the stock, and in some cases, dividends, which occur if the company distributes a portion of its earnings to the owners. Other forms of buying ownership include growth exchange traded funds, real estate, mutual funds, and variable annuities, to name a few. Suffice it to say, there are no guarantees, so researching the quality of the underlying investment is critical. Clearly, the risk is higher when you buy ownership but so is the potential return.

Investors today have a myriad of options to consider, and it is important to actively engage the client in a discussion detailing what you offer and how things would work moving forward.

Wall Street has invented many permutations and commutations of this lend/buy matrix, but when you boil it down, it is that simple—lend money or buy ownership. All well-diversified portfolios have a balance of these two approaches that is developed in accordance with the client's risk tolerance and can be adjusted as markets and the client's circumstances change.

It is recommended that you always ask, throughout this presentation, if what you are saying is understood. On many, many occasions, the client will ask to take the presentation paper home.

Investing 101

Lend	**Buy**
Certificates of deposit	Common stocks
Savings accounts	Growth mutual funds
Fixed return annuities	Growth ETFs
Municipal bonds	Real estate
Corporate bonds	Commodities
Bond ETFs	
Lend: returns are guaranteed (As long as the lender has the resources to meet their obligations)	Buy: returns are variable

Most portfolios are balanced

The planner who elects to work with an established firm will have an investment platform to use in structuring a client's portfolio. The planner who "hangs out his/her own shield" must structure a portfolio with a robust asset allocation divided between lend and own investments, diversified among a variety of assets within each bucket. For example, on the buy side of the ledger: large-cap growth, mid-cap growth, value-oriented securities, emerging markets, small capitalization companies and commodities. It is generally advisable for the planner to use either mutual funds or exchange traded funds to accomplish this diversification coupled with down market protection. It is impossible to cover all of the options to be used in structuring a portfolio in this primer, so the planner should have a "go to" source for help.

The single most important thing to determine prior to structuring a portfolio is the client's risk/reward tolerance. The planner should also provide education on the potential consequences of a market decline with various lend vs. growth allocations. These findings should be fully documented, reviewed regularly with the client and updates made as circumstances change.

Plan Design and Presentation

The necessary documents are in hand, goals have been set, and the plan can now be prepared.

Here are some of the key things to keep in mind when designing a plan:

1. How much free cash flow is available to allocate toward implementing the plan?
2. If cash flow is tight, work with the client to prioritize the allocation. For example, a young couple with small children should be protected against a premature death with the proper amount of life insurance. At this stage, term life insurance (like buying car insurance with the hope someone does not have to collect) may have the most utility. In addition, the most important asset a younger couple has is the ability to earn an income, so protecting that with long-term disability coverage is essential. Lastly, an allocation to a structured savings program is essential, regardless of the amount. Getting into the habit of making regular deposits is an important key in building long-term financial security. Accumulating capital can be important on many fronts, with retirement and the education of children being two primary reasons.
3. On the education of children, the planner should work to determine if the client's offspring would go to a private or state college and for how many years. The costs are readily accessible online, and any quality financial planning software will present the findings nicely. Rates of inflation and rates of return on education savings are key factors in this analysis.
4. In examining the use of available resources, the protection of the family's income with life and disability insurance should come first; accumulating capital for educational purposes and accumulating money for financial independence or retirement are next. The process of accumulating capital has three important components: (a) a reserve for emergency purposes; (b) allocation to the client's employer's retirement plan, IRAs, and other qualified (pretax) retirement vehicles; and (c) allocation to the other elements of the client's financial plan (insurance and investments). Tradeoffs can be made between items (b) and (c), but the idea is to effectively deploy resources in a manner aimed at achieving lifetime financial goals.
5. For the parent or couple concerned about retirement and whose children are already educated, the review and structuring of their investment portfolio, coupled with a calculation of how much needs to be invested to get them to their desired income goal, would be key priorities. There are many variables that enter into this calculation, including when the client wants to retire, assumed investment returns, a discussion about the client's risk/reward tolerance and the influence it has on asset allocation and return, and client living expenses. Another consideration or expense is the potential acquisition of long-term care insurance that will protect the client's assets for the next generation.
6. Occasionally, clients will surface who have sufficient dollars accumulated to achieve their goals. In this instance, the planner will focus on risk/reward tolerance, asset allocation, and management of expectations. It is always helpful to understand why they were dissatisfied with their former advisor. It is also worth noting that many people who come in at this level have investment assets in many different buckets and need help getting organized and consolidating accounts. Many extraordinarily successful relationships emanate from this organization and consolidation process.

7. Clients at every stage of their lives should have an estate plan that directs the distribution of assets in case of death, which can mean a will in the early years and perhaps revocable or irrevocable trusts for the more mature clients. Health care proxies, powers of attorney, and living wills are all necessary at every level. In this regard, it is important for the planner to cultivate relationships with lawyers of varying skill levels—those that are adept at doing simple wills and plans as well as those who have a deeper knowledge and experience with more sophisticated arrangements that might be necessary. If clients have a long-term relationship with an attorney friend who might be a competent lawyer but does not do estate work, suggest that they find someone who does that work specifically and ask the friend to be of counsel. This can be tricky, for sure, but it is also important. In addition, the planner should make sure clients have competent help in the accounting area.

8. The planner will undoubtedly face clients with highly varied estate planning needs which may include one or more of the following:

   a. Making sure a sufficient capital base is available to provide income to the surviving spouse, pay estate expenses and educate children. If one of the spouses is the primary bread-winner, then it is generally advisable to have life insurance on that person to provide for the above. In addition, some insurance on the other spouse to allow for the primary breadwinner to continue to work is important.
   b. If there are young children involved, then setting up a trust for their benefit in the event both parents were to succumb is important. The selection of a guardian and trustee for the trusts is important and can be handled with the estate planning attorney.
   c. A substantial base of capital that would be subject to taxation if/when one or both of the spouses passes away. The clients might be interested in reducing or eliminating these taxes, if possible, and in making sure their legacies are preserved with asset protection mechanisms like trusts.
   d. It is not possible to cover every single situation that a planner might encounter. It is important that the planner know what questions to ask in gathering client data, recognizing what the client might want to accomplish, making suitable recommendations and engaging an attorney for the client (and planner) to work with to help the client meet and accomplish objectives. A diagram that simplifies the decision-making process for the client follows and can serve as a guidepost for follow-up actions.

Estate Flow | 2021

Sample Client

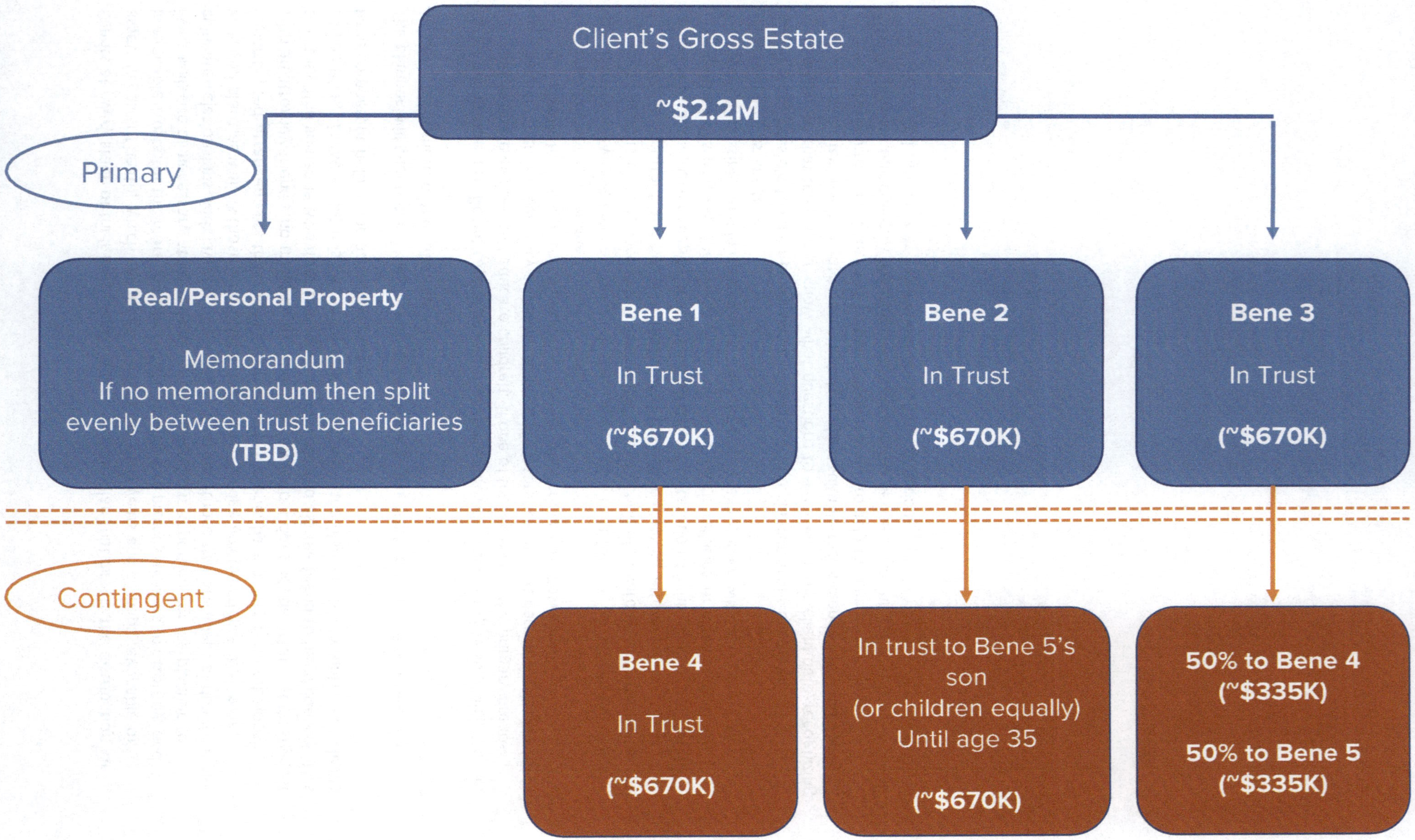

9. The planner should also look at the client's business interests if the person is an owner or partner, with an eye toward contingency planning or what happens when the client cannot work any longer. Simply put, the best advice for a planner dealing with a client who is going to enter any business relationship is to say, "Define how you are going to get out of it before you get in." It makes life so much simpler not to have to negotiate these things after a life-changing event takes place. In addition to this, the owner or partner in a business may have access to retirement plans that allow for the accumulation of capital on a tax-favored basis, at rates greater than those afforded by IRAs and 401(k)s. These are typically referred to as integrated profit-sharing, defined benefit, and cash balance plans. The planner need not be an expert in any of these but should recognize when they might be applicable and then work with a third-party administrator (TPA) to design one that makes sense for the client. Being able to manage investment accounts outside of the ordinary is an important skill to develop, and the client's appreciation for your advice and its implementation is part of the reward.

10. One additional point to help further the process, to the extent it makes sense for your situation, is to have the paperwork ready for implementation of the plan. One the most effective "closes" is very simply saying, "We have the paperwork to put things in place when you are ready to go and can proceed now or at a later date, if you prefer."

Of course, every individual point involved in plan preparation is not covered here. But when the topics outlined above are raised and discussed thoroughly, a solid foundation will be in place for a long-term relationship. If the planner has gained agreement on the client's goals and addresses each one in the plan, closing should be fairly easy. If a client says they want to think about it, then simply ask, "What are you concerned with? Did I miss something? Or is more explanation needed?" The Professional Selling Skills training will be a significant help to the planner in addressing both questions and objections.

Finally, ALWAYS SEND A LETTER RECAPPING WHAT WAS COVERED IN EVERY MEETING. This helps and protects planners in a litigious society and reminds them and the client of all that was said, laying the groundwork for future meetings. A template should be developed to make follow-up document preparation easy, comprehensive, and useful to the client.

Closing

Closing should take place throughout the entire process of developing a long-term financial planning relationship. It is safe to say that every interaction with a potential or actual client should involve a close to end the session. In addition, gaining agreement throughout the entire process makes the final close almost a given. Below are some examples.

During the data-gathering process

- Have I captured that information correctly?
- Does this approach make sense so far?
- Are you comfortable with the process so far?

During the goal-setting process

- Does that accurately reflect your feelings, wishes, and desires?
- Is there anything that we are missing?

After the data gathering and goal setting, tell the client, "We are going to use the information we have gathered to prepare a financial plan aimed at helping you achieve your goals and objectives. However, it is your life, and we want to make sure it works for you, so adjustments can be made, okay? Does that make sense? Are you comfortable with that?"

After getting agreement and buy-in, explain further to the client, "Following the preparation of the plan, we will quarterback the implementation process, including other advisors, like your accountant or attorney, as needed. We will then review progress on a regular basis, say, two or three times annually. Does this make sense to you?"

The financial planner should ALWAYS validate a client's positive response with a "good," "excellent," "great," or "understood," acknowledging the client's agreement.

These questions and subsequent validations are a precursor to "signing the client up," making that process almost automatic. The planner has secured so many agreements along the way that he or she is now in total sync with the client. This series of commitments should not be looked upon as selling but rather as a continual series of "nudges" to get the client engaged and on the right track. The mindset that the planner must have is one that says, "You are doing clients a big favor by getting them on board." Many people will simply let their finances drift if they are not given a clear roadmap to follow with comprehensive and regular follow up.

Implementation and Follow Up

This next step in the process is essential in building a solid, long-term relationship with the client. Once the planner has gained agreement on the points covered in the plan and the resources that can be allocated to the implementation, closing and follow-through are the next steps to be taken.

If the planner is confident that the plan is solid and that the client will agree to going ahead, the easiest close (nudge) is to have the paperwork ready for a signature at the conclusion of the plan presentation. Simply stating that all the paperwork has been prepared if the client is ready to proceed usually results in agreement from the client to continue—and the signature and checks logically follow. When the planner has the necessary implementation documentation in hand, the following steps should occur:

1. Confirm the client's goals and say the paperwork will be processed to begin working toward achieving them.
2. Either provide the client with copies immediately or send them with a follow-up letter.
3. A follow-up letter confirming the actions taken is very reassuring to the client and outlines the next steps.
4. The planner should also review the type of reporting the client can expect and the frequency thereof.
5. Close the meeting by setting another date for the client(s) to visit and asking them to bring along the large amount of paperwork that might be generated through the implementation process. This serves to help the client(s) understand what was sent to them, what they should keep, and what can be thrown away.
6. As always, a follow-up letter after every meeting should be prepared and sent, being sure to address any outstanding questions from the client.

It is ideal for the planner and saves the client a lot of time if the closing can take place immediately following the presentation of the plan. If the paperwork is not prepared or if the client wants to review the plan before implementing, then another meeting will have to be set up for implementation. The immediate presentation of the plan and implementation ensures things will proceed without delay. If the use of an outside advisor is necessary—for example, an attorney to prepare estate documents—then the planner should offer to coordinate that meeting and suggest attending along with the client to ensure that the appropriate topics are addressed.

As stated previously, the planner should develop relationships with attorneys who can put basic estate plans together for most clients as well as for those needing some more sophisticated techniques. Often, clients have not had their estate plans updated to conform with the laws that are in place today and need some prodding to get this done. The addition of children, life insurance to protect the family, the onset of capital accumulation to meet goals, and a variety of personal circumstances unique to each client will need the involvement of an estate planning specialist to make sure the client's estate plan is current.

On many occasions, the planner will hear from a client that some particular attorney "did our house closing, and we liked him a lot, so we can use him here." The planner needs to exercise caution in steering clients to a specialist so as not to discredit a relationship with their current attorney. This is effectively done by asking clients to specifically question their attorney's estate planning expertise. If the expertise is not in evidence, then the clients' regular attorney could be asked to be of counsel in the process. As with most things, the best course of action is not to be a jack of all trades and master of none. Our job is to make sure the estate planning job is done properly for clients by employing the appropriate level of expertise. The planner should also indicate that, as a part of the regular review process, the provisions in their estate plan will be discussed and updates suggested as necessary.

Once the plan is implemented and, if necessary, the estate plan is completed, then the planner should discuss with the client the timetable for follow-up meetings. Some clients may prefer to meet three or four times per year (reserve this for the higher net worth clients with more complicated situations), while others may indicate that only an annual meeting is necessary. The planner needs to guide the client through setting that timetable with statements like "we want to make sure you are properly serviced, and from our point of view, two meetings per year should do it. Do you agree?" These review meetings should be comprehensive—not necessarily long but certainly comprehensive. An agenda is helpful to keep things on track, capturing items such as a review of the client's goals and an investment review that includes asset allocation, performance, market outlook, required minimum distribution status for older clients, review of beneficiaries, and other details that the most recent follow-up letter might trigger.

CAUTION: The matter of beneficiary designations is a detail that the planner must review and follow up on regularly. Insurance policies, annuities, and retirement accounts, to name a few, pass on to the next generation by function of contract (i.e., named beneficiaries) AND NOT BY WILL. The planner should frequently review the appropriateness of previously established designations, as life circumstances for clients often change. Keeping these beneficiary designations current is critical and helps avoid potentially costly legal squabbles following a client's death. If the beneficiaries are minors or people who lack financial acumen or have special circumstances, then a trust should be considered as the direct beneficiary, including provisions to distribute money to the beneficiaries of the trust. This situation requires special treatment and probably needs to be handled by an estate planning specialist.

CAUTION: Compliance standards in the financial industry are very important to adhere to since they are structured to protect both consumers and planners. If planners have any doubts about what they are presenting or if a client is asking for an out-of-bounds favor or activity, planners need to check the compliance implications. It is not worth risking one's career on a sketchy proposition. You can be sure that if your firm is audited by the Securities and Exchange Commission (SEC) or FINRA that planner activities will be reviewed in detail. Stick to your knitting!!! The College for Financial Planning Code of Ethics provides a set of guidelines to follow as well.

The Team Approach

The tendency of financial planners, sometimes referred to as relationship managers, to try and do it all themselves is quite common. As a relationship manager builds a list of clients, the ability to delegate is an essential part of effectively continuing a pattern of growth. To begin with, the myriad of details that surface in servicing clients is endless. In general, taking care of these details is not a productive use of the planner's time. Yes, the buck stops with the planner, so it is critically important for the planner to keep a checklist of outstanding tasks and follow up to make sure they are taken care of, noting the same in the client's file.

The real message here is to build a team that can do the follow up for you. Reliability, effective problem solving, and caring for people are three important skills that all team members should have. The expense of beginning to build a team might seem unnecessary and overwhelming early in the planner's career, but when done effectively, it pays for itself many times over.

An important collateral benefit of building a support team is the learning that the team experiences every day. A new problem becomes an old one in short order since the support team has handled it before. It is vitally important to delegate tasks and problem resolution that the support person might know nothing about. Planners need to provide some guidance as to the approach and then have the support person take it from there and report back to the planner with the results and proposed solutions. When the support person is asked to handle a new subject, task, or area by a client, it is important for building credibility and enhancing the learning process to respond, "I do not know but let me find out and I will get back to you."

All of the above suggestions work to build client confidence in planners and their teams, allow planners time to work on productive business-building endeavors, and serve to properly train the support staff. I gradually built up an excellent staff over my nearly four-decade career in financial services. In what follows, I will go over the basic steps and timeline I utilized.

1. At the end of year one, an administrative assistant was hired who scheduled appointments, typed correspondence, maintained the client files, kept a follow-up list for the planner, opened mail, paid bills, greeted clients when they came in for meetings, provided them with refreshments, maintained the planner's schedule (both personal and business), and painstakingly tracked client investment portfolios.

2. In the second year, as the business grew, a second administrative assistant was hired who took over the process of investing clients' funds as they were received, tracking client investments (manually, if you can believe it), and serving as a backup for the other administrative assistant.

3. At some point in the first three years, the process began of automating portions of the operation with a payroll service (ADP) and, a little later, an investment tracking and report preparation service (Advent). This automation was essential to boosting productivity.

4. It should be noted that I was still heavily involved in the administrative mix, handling things that were not mentioned in points 1–3. In year five, I hired my firm's first plan preparation staff member and did the training from scratch. As the business grew, that person was soon followed by two more plan preparers. Accuracy in capturing client data and in preparing plans is of

paramount importance and at times not understood to the proper degree by new preparers. That problem is quickly solved by asking these preparers to sit in on the meetings while you are presenting. If a mistake surfaces, the preparer quickly learns that it is embarrassing and unacceptable; it usually does not happen again.

5. In the early years, mutual funds were the investment vehicle of choice, and the plan preparers and I would develop the plan and make the investments.

6. Time moved on and the business grew (delegation was a huge key). More operations people were continually added and soon were joined by a dedicated investment person and an executive backup for me that was granted an ownership position. Today, that person is a key player and major owner in the business, with a very significant list of clients.

7. Other additions during this period included a retirement plan development and service team, technology staff (previously outsourced), a compliance officer, a chief financial officer, a chief investment officer, investment analysts, a team of relationship managers with direct support people for them, and a dedicated receptionist. We also now have a marketing team solely focused on business development, presentation materials, responding to requests for proposals, and community relations. Another important person, one not to be minimized, is an office caretaker who is a jack of all trades and takes care of many tasks that surface in our building, even occasionally getting cars washed for the executive team.

8. The most significant personnel move over the years was bringing in an executive who could build on the base that had been created, modernize our approach to everything in the business, be strong in managing client relationships, and carry the business into the future. I am extremely fortunate to have a son with experience in the financial field coupled with a desire to learn every aspect of the business. He began working in the firm 14 years ago, has taken over all day-to-day management tasks, and is innovative in making sure we are ready to tackle the future. Behind him is an eight-years-younger brother and our marketing team manager, who is in the wings along with several other key people, to carry us further into the future.

Please know that the addition of all these people was fostered by delegation, empowering others to do jobs that allowed the relationship managers to focus on business development, and always doing the right thing for our clients.

All this growth was done on a "pay as you go" basis, which has resulted in a completely independent firm. In today's world, people entering the field should undoubtedly have an infrastructure in place to support their work. The principles of delegation and effectively using your support personnel still hold true, though.

In the Face of Adversity

It would certainly be a dream to have a financial planning career that always goes smoothly, with never-failing returns and an unfailing stream of happy clients, but that is an impossibility. Adversity can present itself in several ways, but this chapter will focus on just two of them. The first is a set of circumstances that cause disruption in the financial markets, and the second is dissatisfied clients.

Market Disruptions

1. The crash of 1987 took place on Monday, October 19, and has since been referred to as Black Monday. The Dow Jones average fell by 508 points that day, a decline of 22.6%. This decline was caused by the confluence of several factors, including a market that had been on a bull run for several years (raising price-earnings ratios to unjustifiable highs), inflation rearing its head, the stalling of economic growth, and the introduction of program trading. Program trading is driven by computers that generate sell orders as the market declines. Each time a new price point is reached in the program, more sales occur, resulting in cascading prices. The combination of all these factors caused one very painful experience for many people. This event was the first truly significant market decline since the crash of 1929, and it sent tremors through the markets and investors took a few years to recover. The financial planning community had its first real test in dealing with unsure and skeptical investors. The conventional wisdom did ultimately win out: It was not the time to sell in the face of this precipitous decline but was, in fact, a real buying opportunity.

2. The next significant event took place in late 1999 and early 2000 and was dubbed "the bursting of the Internet bubble." This event sent ripples through the stock market for three years; during 2000, 2001, and 2002, the Dow Jones declined by a total of 30%, and the broader Standard and Poor's 500 average fell by 46.5%—painful indeed. This period of decline was triggered by the rampant speculation that surrounded the increasing prevalence of the Internet and Internet-based companies. Birth was given to company after company, each of which had a better mousetrap. The investing public was captivated by this movement and poured money into a host of companies that were not producing any earnings but had published growth forecasts that predicted significant earnings developing down the road. The incredible gains that were generated for a time in the late 1990s was an incentive for money to pour into the Internet stocks and into other segments of the market as well. The primary driver was plain greed. Fundamentally, a stock price should be reflective of the earnings a company is producing and the prospects for the growth of these earnings. As stated, many of these companies had zero earnings. Yet their stock prices soared—a perfect storm for disaster. The cascading prices of many dot-com stocks rippled from the tech sector through the rest of the market. Many conservative money management companies were under tremendous client pressure to invest in these bubble companies that, in the end, declined in value, with many going out of business. Our firm accommodated the clients who wanted in by setting them up with what we called "play" accounts, putting the risk on the client's shoulders. We had several short-term multimillionaires, and we continually asked them to sell their shares or put the securities in a charitable remainder trust (CRT). Once the securities were owned by the CRT, shares could be sold with a minimal tax impact, and the client could take an income for life. Not one person elected to go the CRT route because an irrational sense of optimism convinced them that these stocks were going to go much higher. Yeah, right! If only people invested in and stuck with

Microsoft. Financial planners learned a very valuable lesson, which was to recommend and stay with diversified portfolios of securities whose value could be supported by solid underlying fundamentals.

3. Following the bursting of the dot-com bubble, the market experienced six years of solid growth. In October of 2008, that period came to a dramatic end with the onset of the 2008 fiscal crisis. The driving factor in this crisis was speculation in the mortgage market. Mortgage loans were given to the public in substantial amounts through banks and other types of lending institutions. At the same time, housing prices were rising, and the standards for issuing mortgages were loosened considerably. In many cases, mortgages were given to people who were not good credit risks, resulting in many substandard loans. The next turn of events involved the institutions packaging these mortgages in instruments like mortgage-backed securities (MBS) and collateralized mortgage obligations (CMBS). The safety of these packages was touted; in fact, many were rated AAA because they were diversified and had the value of the mortgaged houses as security. Sounded good, it seemed. Well, not so much, as it turned out. Houses stopped rising in value and, in fact, began to decline. The buyers who had mortgages were often underwater (that is, the values of their houses were often lower than the mortgages). The homeowners were stuck with their homes and the mortgage payments attached to them. As a result, the underlying mortgage payors began defaulting on their outsized obligations. As the default rate escalated, with more occurring every day, the value of the underlying houses continued to decline. This entire problem was worsened by the sale of credit default swaps, which theoretically served as insurance against the collapse of MBS and CMO securities. Huge bets were placed on these credit default swaps, and while the story is complicated, things did not work out for these investors as the underlying market deteriorated. As a result, defaults on mortgages and the forced sale of distressed real estate put pressure on other assets that had to be sold to meet obligations coming due. The sweeping impact of all the above hit the stock market extremely hard, with a decline of 38% in 2008, coupled with a severe disruption in the fixed income market, as the entire banking system was on the verge of collapse. Enter the federal government with bailouts for the banks that were deemed to be "too big to fail." The system began to right itself, and the crisis was shortened with the input of federal stimulus. The deregulation of the financial markets was a primary driver in this collapse since easy mortgage money was available for housing that had rising prices, providing an incentive for people to speculate. This was all coupled with the eagerness of the institutions to make these loans in their quest for outsized profits. The final result was another bubble bursting. Greed ruled again. Following the narrow escape from the 2008 crisis, legislation was introduced to regulate financial markets. In the end, the Dodd-Frank Wall Street Reform and Consumer Protection Act was passed to improve accountability and transparency in the financial system. It included "too big to fail" bailouts and offered protection for consumers from abusive financial services practices. Quality and diversification again ruled the day in the financial planning community.

4. Once the 2008 monetary crisis was in the rearview mirror, a period of financial peace and tranquility followed. Then in late 2019, quietly emerging in a place quite remote from the United States, in the city of Wuhan, China (yet to be proven as of this writing), a silent but deadly virus was born: COVID-19, more commonly called the coronavirus. Around 80,000 cases quickly surfaced in China and, with a global economy supported by international mobility, the virus began to spread rampantly. This highly contagious virus took a while to reach the shores of the United States, but when it did, the spread was pervasive. Medical professionals and treatment facilities were put under tremendous pressure while treating COVID-19 patients. Many cases emanated from cruise ship passengers and people coming to the US from foreign countries,

primarily East Asia. It took the United States some time to react to this new development, primarily because it was hard to fathom how potent it was—at least that is what many people thought. The death toll in the United States has exceeded 600,000, with 3.86 million lives lost worldwide. The specter of the virus caused a significant short-term downturn in the stock market (20%) because the economic impact was so uncertain. Then a significant rebound occurred, with the Standard and Poor's 500 rising 60+% from the end of March 2020 through June 15 of 2021. The COVID-19 chapter of our history is still being written with the onset of the delta variant, but since the onset, treatment regimens have been substantially improved, several vaccines have been brought to market, and the impact of the virus is waning a bit as of this writing.

5. There have been several other instances of adversity that, while severe, generally had relatively short-lived fiscal impacts. While the 9/11/2001 terrorist attack was horrific, the various markets affected stabilized rather quickly, and we moved forward.

The long and the short of these periods of adversity is that the investing public appreciates a steady hand on the wheel to take impulsive moves out of the equation. In addition, maintaining a well-diversified portfolio of high-quality securities and sticking with it has generally proven to be in the best interest of a planner's clients.

Dissatisfied Clients

The second form of disruption that causes serious strife in the life of a planner is the dissatisfied client. The level of dissatisfaction can vary, but it is usually short term in nature, and corrective measures can be put in place to right the ship almost immediately. On occasion, the client can take it to the next level by filing a complaint with FINRA, the Financial Industry Regulatory Authority, and after that engage an attorney to air grievances through the process of arbitration, seeking monetary remuneration. To say this is disconcerting for the planner is a huge understatement. You have put your best foot forward with the client and made every effort to serve him or her, but sometimes that simply is not enough, and the client acts. Without question, though, the entire process of working through an errors and omissions attorney to get a case settled is stressful and mentally disruptive. It is a constant back-of-the-mind weight that hangs over the day-to-day financial planning process. It is vital that the planner take immediate steps when confronted with a dissatisfied client to address the situation as soon as it arises; do not try to sweep it under the rug. Make every effort to solve the problem from the outset, and make sure any complaints are reported to your firm's compliance officer.

Avoiding Adversity and Minimizing Disruptions

To keep this simple, the steps taken to avoid adversity and minimize disruptions are presented in outline form and provide a solid template for developing successful client relationships. The bulk of complaints from dissatisfied clients arise from investment returns that do not meet their expectations. As outlined below, defining expectations can forestall many potential complaints. Simply stated, if you have done your job well, it is far better for the client to stay the course in almost every instance of adversity.

1. Take great care to understand the client's personal and financial situation. Throughout that process, begin to get a sense of the client's attitude toward risk and sensitivity to market fluctuations. Document your findings in a letter to the client.

2. Make sure to establish goals that you and the client plan to work together to achieve. Confirm and reconfirm your findings verbally, documenting them in letters to the client.
3. When putting the initial plan together and presenting it to the client, reconfirm your findings in points one and two.
4. In structuring an investment portfolio, it makes sense to do an elasticity test on the recommended fixed versus growth balance. To translate this, if the recommended mix is 60% growth and 40% fixed, what kinds of gains and losses can the client expect with various market fluctuations? Confirm what you agreed to in writing. Document!
5. Particularly for older clients, take great care in determining how much liquidity is available for emergencies, what their living expenses are, and whether there are any large expenses on the horizon. What often makes the most sense is creating a silo in the client's investment mix that has a cash reserve for what was just outlined. This might include, say, two years' worth of expenses. This reserve, in combination with dividends and interest, will usually give the clients two and one-half years of a cushion and assurance that they will be able to meet their living expenses without selling in a down market. Keeping this mix in place is essential. Document!
6. For younger people, encourage them to build toward having that liquid reserve while investing the bulk of their free cash flow for the longer term. In this case, we suggest that cash to support six months of living expenses be available. Younger people who are employed have time to recover from a bad market. In fact, they should welcome it, as they can buy investment assets at reduced prices.

The overriding issue looked at in FINRA arbitration cases is often that of suitability—that is, were the investments suitable for the client's situation and/or risk/reward tolerance? Focus heavily on the first and second points of this section to address the suitability issue carefully for each client. The extra time it takes to do this at the onset of a relationship will be well worth it in the final analysis. If an advisor is acting in the capacity of a fiduciary, then other considerations may be brought to bear in a FINRA Arbitration case.

In consideration of the four major financial system disruptions described in the first section of this chapter, there are several things to do to help clients deal with similar scenarios. The essential keys in managing through adversity are to set aside an adequate liquid reserve to allow the client to weather the crisis, determine in advance whether the client has the "stomach" to stand the market volatility and declines, and frequently communicate these findings to the client, accompanied by documentation. To repeat, liquidity requirements and portfolio elasticity need to be covered on a regular basis with the client during normal reviews. In addition, when the disruption occurs, frequent communications with the client are essential and should re-emphasize the important points outlined above.

To reiterate three especially important points in this section, be careful and thorough in your fact-finding; document, document, document; and advise the client to stay the course during periods of disruption.

Case Studies

Financial planners have the opportunity to work on a wide variety of interesting cases during their career. Every single case has its own nuances and requires frequent reviews and updates as the client relationship progresses. It might be helpful to review three specific types of cases, each with different sets of challenges: the young couple, the family business, and the retiree. These cases are not real but do parallel situations I have experienced during my career. The data gathering process and listening to what the clients have to say are essential to developing a plan of action. In every case that follows, the setting of goals and continued work toward those goals was essential to the process.

Case studies presented are based on actual clients; however, some of the information may have been changed or altered. These studies are provided for educational purposes only. Similar, or even positive results, cannot be guaranteed. Each client has their own unique set of circumstances so products and strategies may not be suitable for all people. Please consult with a qualified professional before implementing any strategy discussed herein.

No portion of these case studies is to be interpreted as a testimonial or endorsement of the author's or his firm's, investment advisory services.

The Young Couple

Thirty years ago, a young physician and his spouse decided to begin planning their finances and engaged our firm to work with them. The couple had two small children and were just beginning to see the medical practice produce income over and above what was needed to meet day-to-day expenses. After compiling an inventory of the client's assets and developing a complete personal profile, we went through the process of setting goals to work toward. Planning for financial independence, educating their children, protecting the family in the event of death or disability, and transferring assets to the survivor, and ultimately to the next generation in the event of death, were determined to be our starting points.

The clients had $1500 per month in income that could be allocated to the planning process. In this case, protecting the family in the event of death or disability were the top priorities, as the physician's income was their biggest asset, and it needed to be protected. A substantial but inexpensive term life insurance policy was secured on the physician to provide income for the spouse in the event of death. A term insurance policy was also secured for the physician's spouse to provide funds to care for the children if she were to die prematurely. In addition, an income disability replacement policy was secured so that income would continue in the event that the physician was unable to work due to an accident or illness. The remaining dollars were allocated to education accounts and personal savings to work toward accumulating what our forecasts called for in each area. There was not enough to fund all these goals at this stage of the clients' lives, but we knew that the income would grow, and more dollars could be allocated to their plan in the future.

In addition, we met with an attorney to develop an estate plan and create documents that were aimed at having assets passed to the surviving adult, and ultimately their children, in a manner that made them comfortable. There were numerous twists and turns in the planning for these clients that were dealt with by meeting regularly (3 or 4 times per year) and sending follow-up letters detailing what changes were being made in order to meet their goals.

These clients rigorously followed the direction we worked together to establish throughout the entire process. Today, they have accumulated $14 million through a variety of qualified retirement plans and nonqualified accounts; two children were educated, one for 6 years; their disability insurance was dropped; and $3,000,000 in survivorship life insurance, owned by an irrevocable life insurance trust, was taken out to pay estate taxes before the unified credit was reset to current levels. Throughout the years, we have worked with legal counsel to revise their estate plan several times, adjust savings levels, update beneficiary designations, and manage assets in a conservative, tax-efficient manner. The keys to this were clients who were committed to the plan and the very regular reviews and updates provided over the years. What a great feeling it is to have things develop like this for both the clients and planner.

The Family Business

As stated earlier, the best business arrangements begin by carefully defining, before you enter a relationship, how you are going to get out in the event of death, disability, or retirement. In this case, we were dealing with a business started a generation ago by the current owner's great-grandfather. We entered the relationship when the current owner's son took over the company and recognized the importance of a plan that could protect his family and that of his son, who would be the next owner.

We worked with legal counsel to construct a shareholder's agreement that defined how the current owner would get out of the business in the event that any of the problems mentioned above were to come to pass. An important part of the agreement was to develop a company valuation methodology that accurately reflected what the owner and his son felt was reasonable. The accounting firm worked through several iterations before we settled on a reasonable value. It should be noted that any business owner might have two values in mind. The first is often tied to what the owner might want if someone walked through the front door and offered to write a check for the business, in which case a higher value might be conceived by the owner. The second is what the owner would use for estate valuation purposes and in transferring shares to a new generation. The result of this is generally a lower value that can be substantiated with a formula.

Once the current owner decided to begin transitioning out of the business, the gifting of a modest number of shares to his son on a regular basis commenced, and a life insurance policy was obtained on both the father and the son so that shares could be transferred without jeopardizing the financial stability of the company in the event of the death of either party. Both the father/owner and son worked side by side for years until the father ultimately retired. The buy and sell/shareholder's agreement allowed for a comfortable transition of the shares to his son, using a combination of gifting, share purchases, a consulting agreement, and a supplemental retirement plan.

Fast forward to today, and the same arrangement has been worked out for the great-great-grandson of the original founder. All of this required extensive help from legal counsel, regular reviews, and consistent updates. As an aside, we manage the personal investment accounts for the entire family as well as the company retirement plan. Regular reviews and updates and the client's willingness to participate in the planning process were again the keys to making this work.

The Retiree

Recently, an investment "do-it-yourselfer" couple came to see us with a desire to get organized for their upcoming retirement. They had been employed in several businesses over the years and retained their retirement plan balances, had investment accounts in many locations, and had an asset allocation pattern without rhyme or reason. Our job involved several key aspects. First, we had to prepare a master list of all their accounts to understand where they were and the kind of values they had. Using this overview, we then had to break it down further to understand how they were diversified, going beyond the fixed and variable asset allocation mix to see how each classification was diversified. The most important aspects of the entire process were determining the clients' risk/reward tolerance, the retirement income they required, and the management strategy for income taxes in the withdrawal process.

Asset class decisions then had to be made, e.g., taxable versus tax-free bonds and the length of maturities in the fixed-return area. On the growth side, the allocation among conservative, moderately aggressive, aggressive, emerging markets, and inflation-hedged securities had to be determined. After these decisions were made, we then had to make sure the consolidation of the various accounts and the repositioning of the portfolio was done in a manner to minimize or spread out the taxes that would be owed in the process.

The closing consisted of reviewing the goals and needs of the clients, confirming our findings, and describing the repositioning we were recommending. In a case like this, there are always client questions due to the complexities of the situation. The keys here were clearly defining and gaining agreement on what the client wanted to accomplish, preparing the paperwork necessary to implement the changes, getting the paperwork signed, and following through on its processing, keeping the client informed throughout. A meeting was held 30 to 45 days later to review the paperwork the client received during the transition, set them up with online access, and review the new consolidated investment account reports.

Beyond this, it was vitally important for us to review and modify beneficiary arrangements (as they were in a state of disorder), structure their income withdrawals, and help them determine taxes owed on the withdrawals. Later, estate planning was addressed, and a completely updated and modernized plan was prepared. Lastly, the subject of long-term care was reviewed, and action taken to protect the clients. The clients feel much better about everything investment-related, are relieved not to have to keep track of things, and are looking forward to the regular review process that is so central to our service. The follow-up letters we sent were the icing on the cake.

One crucial point that gets at something very typical in a client relationship is that if both spouses are involved in the process, often only one of the two is actually undertaking the day-to-day management of the couple's finances. Setting up a plan with goals and solutions provides both people with a real sense of comfort that, if something were to happen to one of them, the survivor would be protected and assisted by the planner. This often is a key selling point.

A potential "do-it-yourselfer" buried in paperwork and an unorganized situation.

Succession Planning

It is very important for planners to have a succession plan in place that calls for the continuation of their practice if the planner is no longer able to work. Three primary reasons are to allow planners and/or their families to realize a value for the practice, to protect the clients who rely on the planners for service and protect the employees who are working for the planners.

The concept of developing a succession plan can be complex but ought to include two fundamental ingredients:

1. A method for valuing the financial planning practice
2. Absent selling the practice to an unrelated outside buyer, identify one or more individuals in the firm who might purchase the practice

An agreement should be crafted to include both the planner selling the business and the buyer. To protect both the buyer and seller, the terms of the succession plan should be very well-defined, including valuation methodology and payment terms. Often, the agreement is "funded" with life insurance so that a part or the entire buyout can be completed in the event of death of either the seller or buyer. The terms of the agreement should also provide for the transition of ownership in the event of a total and permanent disability, which can be insured as well. Retirement provisions are often left out, and a death- or disability-only agreement is used in the early, more formative years. When the planner nears retirement, then the full range of transition options can be explored.

Legal counsel should be employed to protect both the potential seller and buyer, and the parties to the agreement should review the plan annually. There are a lot of twists and turns that can develop in the succession planning process, so it is very important to continually review the arrangement to keep it current. The planner's clients will take comfort in knowing that a solid succession plan is in place, thus ensuring that their interests will be taken care of now and on into the future. Hence, it makes a great deal of sense to communicate the plan to the clients as well as the employees of the firm in order to provide them a sense of comfort and security.

The very last point to consider is the involvement of others in the ownership of equity in the firm. To construct an effective succession plan, it may be necessary to involve the potential buyer as an equity owner. The potential buyer can own stock outright or in the form of phantom shares.

To repeat, the complexities of this process, just like those on which you are advising your clients, are many and varied. An experienced business lawyer should be engaged from the beginning, and the planner should thoroughly review all available options in the succession planning process. This short chapter is just the tip of the succession planning iceberg. Conversations on the subject with a business attorney and accountant will absolutely be necessary.

GOOD LUCK!

Epilogue

The number of concepts presented in this guide will not be useful or applicable to every planner and every situation. However, I hope that some of the ideas and concepts can help you develop your practice in this extremely rewarding field. The enjoyment that is derived by continually helping a broad range of clientele is the best reward possible. Yes, the financial rewards of a planning career can be substantial, but the planner must embody the spirit of helping others to be truly gratified and enjoy waking up every day anxious to get to work.

Appendix Part A

The Dow Jones Industrial Average Values over Time

Date	Value
January 2, 1900	68.13
December 30, 1904	70.05
December 31, 1909	99.05
December 31, 1914	54.58
January 2, 1920	108.76
January 2, 1925	121.25
January 2, 1930	244.20
January 2, 1935	104.51
January 2, 1940	151.43
January 2, 1945	152.58
December 30, 1949	200.52
December 30, 1955	488.40
December 30, 1960	615.89
December 31, 1965	969.26
December 31, 1970	838.92
December 31, 1975	852.41
January 2, 1980	824.57
January 2, 1985	1,198.87
January 2, 1990	2,810.15
February 23, 1995	4,003.33
December 31, 1999	11,497.12
December 31, 2004	10,783.01
December 31, 2009	10,428.05
January 2, 2015	17,832.99
December 31, 2019	28,455.09
December 31, 2020	30,409.56

The Dow Jones Industrial Averages displayed here represent the aggregate of just 30 blue chip common stocks. As a result, it is not an accurate reflection of the broader markets, including international companies and many smaller and emerging market entities. It does give a sense of the growth that has taken place over many years, though. Today, we live in an age of global interdependence, rapidly evolving technology, and many countries developing modern ways of operating, which result in a very broad range of investment opportunities.

Appendix Part B

The Laws That Govern the Securities Industry

Note: Except as otherwise noted, the links to the securities laws below are from Statute Compilations maintained by the Office of the Legislative Counsel, US House of Representatives. These links are provided for the user's convenience and may not reflect all recent amendments. Full text of all documents is easily found on the Internet. If you havequestions concerning the meaning or application of a particular law, please consult with an attorney who specializes in securities law.

- Securities Act of 1933
- Securities Exchange Act of 1934
- Trust Indenture Act of 1939
- Investment Company Act of 1940
- Investment Advisers Act of 1940
- Sarbanes-Oxley Act of 2002
- Dodd-Frank Wall Street Reform and Consumer Protection Act of 2010
- Jumpstart Our Business Startups Act of 2012

Securities Act of 1933

Often referred to as the "truth in securities" law, the Securities Act of 1933 has two basic objectives:

- require that investors receive financial and other significant information concerning securities being offered for public sale; and
- prohibit deceit, misrepresentations, and other fraud in the sale of securities.

See the full text of the Securities Act of 1933.

Purpose of Registration

A primary means of accomplishing these goals is the disclosure of important financial information through the registration of securities. This information enables investors, not the government, to make informed judgments about whether to purchase a company's securities. While the SEC requires that the information provided be accurate, it does not guarantee it. Investors who purchase securities and suffer losses have important recovery rights if they can prove that there was incomplete or inaccurate disclosure of essential information.

The Registration Process

In general, securities sold in the US must be registered. The registration forms companies file provide essential facts while minimizing the burden and expense of complying with the law. In general, registration forms call for:

- a description of the company's properties and business activities.
- a description of the security to be offered for sale by the company.
- information about the management of the company; and
- financial statements certified by independent accountants.

Registration statements and prospectuses become public shortly after filing with the SEC. If filed by US domestic companies, the statements are available on the EDGAR database accessible at www.sec.gov. Registration statements are subject to examination for compliance with disclosure requirements. Not all offerings of securities must be registered with the Commission. Some exemptions from the registration requirement include:

- private offerings to a limited number of persons or institutions.
- offerings of limited size.
- intrastate offerings; and
- securities of municipal, state, and federal governments.

By exempting many small offerings from the registration process, the SEC seeks to foster capital formation by lowering the cost of offering securities to the public.

Securities Exchange Act of 1934

With this Act, Congress created the Securities and Exchange Commission. The Act empowers the SEC with broad authority over all aspects of the securities industry. This includes the power to register, regulate, and oversee brokerage firms, transfer agents, and clearing agencies as well as the nation's securities self-regulatory organizations (SROs). The various securities exchanges, such as the New York Stock Exchange, the NASDAQ Stock Market, and the Chicago Board of Options are SROs. The Financial Industry Regulatory Authority (FINRA) is also an SRO. N

The Act also identifies and prohibits certain types of conduct in the markets and provides the Commission with disciplinary powers over regulated entities and persons associated with them.

The Act also empowers the SEC to require periodic reporting of information by companies with publicly traded securities.

See the full text of the Securities Exchange Act of 1934.

Corporate Reporting

Companies with more than $10 million in assets whose securities are held by more than 500 owners must file annual and other periodic reports. These reports are available to the public through the SEC's EDGAR database.

Proxy Solicitations

The Securities Exchange Act also governs the disclosure in materials used to solicit shareholders' votes in annual or special meetings held for the election of directors and the approval of other corporate actions. This information, contained in proxy materials, must be filed with the Commission in advance of any solicitation to ensure compliance with the disclosure rules. Solicitations, whether by management or shareholder groups, must disclose all key facts concerning the issues on which holders are asked to vote.

Tender Offers

The Securities Exchange Act requires disclosure of essential information by anyone looking to buy more than 5 percent of a company's securities by direct purchase or tender offer. Such an offer often is extended to gain control of the company. As with the proxy rules, this allows shareholders to make informed decisions on these critical corporate events.

Insider Trading

The securities laws broadly prohibit fraudulent activities of any kind in connection with the offer, purchase, or sale of securities. These provisions are the basis for many types of disciplinary actions, including actions against fraudulent insider trading. Insider trading is illegal when a person trades a security while in possession of material nonpublic information in violation of a duty to withhold the information or refrain from trading.

Registration of Exchanges, Associations, and Others

The Act requires a variety of market participants to register with the Commission, including exchanges, brokers and dealers, transfer agents, and clearing agencies. Registration for these organizations involves filing disclosure documents that are updated on a regular basis.

The exchanges and the Financial Industry Regulatory Authority (FINRA) are identified as self-regulatory organizations (SRO). SROs must create rules that allow for disciplining members for improper conduct and for establishing measures to ensure market integrity and investor protection. SRO-proposed rules are subject to SEC review and published to solicit public comment. While many SRO-proposed rules are effective upon filing, some are subject to SEC approval before they can go into effect.

Trust Indenture Act of 1939

This Act applies to debt securities such as bonds, debentures, and notes that are offered for public sale. Even though such securities may be registered under the Securities Act, they may not be offered for sale to the public unless a formal agreement between the issuer of bonds and the bondholder, known as the trust indenture, conforms to the standards of this Act.

See the full text of the Trust Indenture Act of 1939.

Investment Company Act of 1940

This Act regulates the organization of companies, including mutual funds, that engage primarily in investing, reinvesting, and trading in securities, and whose own securities are offered to the investing public. The regulation is designed to minimize conflicts of interest that arise in these complex operations. The Act requires these companies to disclose their financial condition and investment policies to investors when stock is initially sold and, later, on a regular basis. The focus of this Act is on disclosure to the investing public of information about the fund and its investment objectives, as well as on investment company structure and operations. It is important to remember that the Act does not allow the SEC to directly supervise the investment decisions or activities of these companies or judge the merits of their investments.

See the full text of the Investment Company Act of 1940.

Investment Advisers Act of 1940

This law regulates investment advisers. With certain exceptions, this Act requires that firms or sole practitioners compensated for advising others about securities investments must register with the SEC and conform to regulations designed to protect investors. Since the Act was amended in 1996 and 2010, generally only advisers who have at least $100 million of assets under management or advise a registered investment company must register with the Commission.

See the full text of the Investment Advisers Act of 1940.

Sarbanes-Oxley Act of 2002

On July 30, 2002, President George W. Bush signed into law the Sarbanes-Oxley Act of 2002, which he characterized as "the most far-reaching reforms of American business practices since the time of Franklin Delano Roosevelt." The Act mandated a number of reforms to enhance corporate responsibility, enhance financial disclosures and combat corporate and accounting fraud, and created the "Public Company Accounting Oversight Board," also known as the PCAOB, to oversee the activities of the auditing profession. (Please check the Classification Tables maintained by the US House of

Representatives Office of the Law Revision Counsel for updates to any of the laws.) You can find links to all Commission rulemaking and reports issued under the Sarbanes-Oxley Act at: http://www.sec.gov/spotlight/sarbanes-oxley.htm.

See the full text of the Sarbanes-Oxley Act of 2002.

Dodd-Frank Wall Street Reform and Consumer Protection Act of 2010

The Dodd-Frank Wall Street Reform and Consumer Protection Act was signed into law on July 21, 2010 by President Barack Obama. The legislation set out to reshape the US regulatory system in a number of areas including, but not limited to, consumer protection, trading restrictions, credit ratings, regulation of financial products, corporate governance and disclosure, and transparency. (Please check the Classification Tables maintained by the US House of Representatives Office of the Law Revision Counsel for updates to any of the laws.) You can find links to all Commission rulemaking and reports issued under the Dodd-Frank Act at: http://www.sec.gov/spotlight/dodd-frank.shtml.

See the full text of the Dodd-Frank Wall Street Reform and Consumer Protection Act of 2010.

Jumpstart Our Business Startups Act of 2012

The Jumpstart Our Business Startups Act (the "JOBS Act") was enacted on April 5, 2012. The JOBS Act aims to help businesses raise funds in public capital markets by minimizing regulatory requirements. The full text of the Act is available at: http://www.gpo.gov/fdsys/pkg/BILLS-112hr3606enr/pdf/BILLS-112hr3606enr.pdf. (Please check the Classification Tables maintained by the US House of Representatives Office of the Law Revision Counsel for updates to any of the laws.)

Note: See also Researching the Federal Securities Laws Through the SEC Website.

Appendix Part C

The World's Most Famous Kiss – Photo by Alfred Eisenstaedt

Notes

Notes

Notes